OWN *your* DAY
WITH
FENG SHUI

Cure The Chaos With Seven
Daily Practices & The Secret Of Chi

MARK KIEN SIN

"One who is happiest finds peace
and harmony at home"

~ Chinese Proverb

Seven Daily Practices To Own Your Day

CONTENTS

PART I
THE SECRET OF CHI - FENG SHUI

PART II
CURING THE CHAOS

PART III
SEVEN DAILY PRACTICES TO OWN YOUR DAY

AUTHORS NOTE

Before we begin, there is something you should know... This book is not about ancient mystical energy, or how to rearrange your furniture for good fortune. What this book is about, is real applications, it's physics and mindset, it's about owning each day with simplicity and fulfillment using practical and achievable methods. By the time you finish reading it, you'll be able to adapt your way of thinking and harmonise the space around you. In this book I give you daily practices to help you live life with a more positive, productive and happy environment. What I share is based on my own experiences and a decade of knowledge on how to create awareness of thoughts and feelings to manage life in it's ups and downs, by using the power of your thoughts, energy and vibration in combination with the practice of Feng Shui. By learning about this powerful combination, you'll be introduced to an essential tool, for a life of greater peace and harmony, productivity and happiness. This knowledge and wisdom will help you discover the real power of positive energy and how it can help you create clarity, focus and alignment. Just as the power of thoughts can impact the outcome of your life, so too the power of the space you reside in.

INTRODUCTION

You may have experienced life, feeling like you're not living with full purpose or you're not where you want to be in terms of your career, life mission, money or self-worth. Maybe the frustration is in your home, in your relationships or within the way you look and feel about your body or health. It could even be that you haven't travelled enough or helped enough people, lacked a social life, or creativity and fun. Perhaps you couldn't find the time to learn new skills or a moment to rest. The good news is, it's in your control to identify the areas you hold value to the most and seek balance and fulfillment. If you feel that your life is completely fulfilled, then maybe this book isn't for you right now, if so, please pass it on to someone who you believe would benefit from it. However if you feel that there is room to enhance even just one area of your life, it's important you read on, for what you are about to learn could change your life forever.

It is said that without desire we lack the spark of motivation, we get confused and uncertain about the future which leads to feeling frustrated, fearful and overwhelmed. Now, let's imagine living life with a purpose and true identity, in an environment that brings you joy each and every day. Imagine yourself feeling healthy and strong, building and nurturing relationships with integrity and compassion. Imagine being able to block out the b.s propaganda and surround yourself with positive influences, instead of being cornered by concerns. Imagine living life in peace, harmony and in a carefree manner.

Sounds good isn't it? Then here comes the challenge....

We tried thinking positively, setting goals, turning off the TV, yet in some mysterious way the negative energy that lingers around us creeps in and steals the joy.

I've been in this place, I know the struggle well, and the good news is that there's a way to bypass this negative energy, and you'll need two things in order to achieve it. A structured daily practice that aligns your mental space, and an environment that harmonises the physical space you live/work in.

Boom!

So where should we begin? With some form of meditation, or placing a magic crystal in your home for good luck? Perhaps organising your work space or house with a new sofa or fresh lick of paint? Close but not quite. What if you practiced a structured daily routine that aligns the positive mental space i.e your mindset, and created the positive physical space you live in, to align with this mindset "Hmmm" you say. Let me explain…

In the future would it help if…

- You had better sleep, and created essential morning practices to help you start your day with joy?

- You were clear on your goals and had positive affirmations to help you succeed?

- You could be efficient with your time and be able to rest and reset without being less productive?

- You could spark the motivation to consistently achieve your goals and live with inspiration?

- You could find and understand ultimately the true meaning of life?

This book will help you do just that. The journey for you has just begun and if you practice the secrets this book teaches you, what you'll learn will enhance, if not change your life completely. Within this book you will learn and understand the power of the energy within you, Chi, how to use this energy to manage your thoughts and emotions to bring joy into your life. You'll learn to use the principles of Feng Shui, an ancient Chinese practice to ensure your space flows abundantly with positive energy. You'll learn how to incorporate the five key elements representing water, wood, fire, earth and metal within your home or work. You will learn the meaning of energy balance, Yin and Yang. You will master the areas of life which you value the most within the nine life areas. You will learn seven daily practices to help you own your day with more peace, efficiency and happiness.

PART I

The Secret Of Chi - Feng Shui

Energy Is Chi

Chi

Chi is a vital force that completely surrounds us and our environment. In ancient times, it was referred to as the "dragon's cosmic breath" which has the power to mold into its surroundings. Chi is energy, Chi is universal, which means it's all around us, it surrounds us and makes up everything in the universe. Chi embraces all manifestations of energy, from the most material aspects of energy (such as the earth beneath your feet, this book, and flesh and blood of every living thing) to the most non-material aspects (light, movement, heat, nerve impulses, thoughts and emotions). Chi is in a state of continuous motion, transforming endlessly from one aspect of energy into another. You don't create it nor can you destroy it; it simply changes in its manifestation. When the Qi of your home and yourself are attuned to one another, there is a harmonious flow that is established, making you feel at ease and happy. In the practice of Feng Shui, the goal is to amplify good Chi (Sheng Qi) and to eliminate bad Chi, negativity, or unfortunate luck (Shar Qi). Life, it is said in the Chinese medical classics, is a gathering of Chi. A healthy and happy human being is a dynamic but harmonious mixture of all the aspects of Chi that make up who we are.

Vibration

If you have ever read the book "The Secret" this book identifies and explains "The Law of Attraction" which is ultimately about using the power of your thoughts to manifest what you want in life. Your thoughts are frequencies that send out signals to the universe making it possible for you to attract things you want into your life like a magnet. With this in mind, this law is only a secondary law. There is another law, a primary law being "The Law of Vibration".

To explain this simply, everything is an expression of the same thing: the plants, the trees, the floor, the human body, the clothes. It is all energy at different rates of vibration. Your body is a biological structure with a very high speed of vibration, while your brain is an electronic switching station. Your brain does not think, it's you who actually think with your brain. As you activate brain cells, you set up a vibration in your body. For you to move a part of your body, you have to activate brain cells or that part of your body would not move. Vibration is something that must be understood if you're about to take control of your health, your relationships, business or any areas of your life. If you want to own your day, understanding the law of vibration is essential.

Imagine yourself as a radio frequency tower sending out signals every second of the day and night, with these signals being your thoughts and feelings. What you project out is what you reflect back in. If you feel stressed all day, not only does it bring your mood down, it sets up your frequency vibration and if you don't shift this vibration, you're going to attract more things that stress you out. How you feel is a projection of what you're thinking. You see, it's impossible to feel sad if you are thinking happy thoughts. Try it for a second, take a moment to think of something that really makes you smile and then ask yourself how you feel. The aim is to stay in tune with your thoughts and feelings and maintain good Chi. Of course it's easier said than done, it's almost impossible to have positive thoughts projecting out every second of the day. It takes practice and reputation to be aware of your thoughts. If you can just practice awareness and be in tune to how you are feeling throughout the day and find ways to shift your mood to a positive one, then you're winning.

Energy Projection

Have you ever walked into a room smiling, - guess what, - you most likely got a smile back. It's all because our energy is contagious, it's amazing to see how some people can just light up a room while others can totally dampen it. It's also interesting, we gel with certain people and not with others. It's all about the power of the energy you carry, it is the Chi within you.

Our thoughts and feelings receive and send thousands of signals each day. The energy you project can also affect other living things around you, not just people. Scientists have acutely measured the effects of energy with organic life showing that mild vibrations increase growth in plants while harsher, stronger vibrations have a negative effect. Basically if you scream and shout around your plants all day the vibrations or Chi could affect their growth. Positive vibrations improve communication and photosynthesis, which improves growth and the ability to fight infection. We could simply say the plants are happier if you're happier. In fact this works with people and animals around you too. If you have a dog, you will notice how their mood can mirror your feelings. Dogs are highly intuitive and can sense your vibrations before you even do.

Another fun fact about the law of vibration... A Japanese 'doctor of alternative medicine' once claimed to be able to think good or bad thoughts when looking at a glass of water and form appealing or ugly ice crystals. He claimed that, depending on the nature of the speech or thoughts directed at the water, when the water is frozen its crystals will be "beautiful" or "ugly" depending on whether the thoughts were positive or negative. If he is right, we have a most amazing phenomenon here with dramatic implications, as known by the simple fact that 70 per cent of all biological tissue, including the human body, is water. The experiments involve exposing glasses of water to various words, pictures or music, then freezing the water and examining the frozen crystals under a microscope. The doctor claimed that positive words and emotions, classical music and positive prayer directed at the water produced beautiful crystals, while negative words and emotions and crude music, such as heavy metal, produced ugly crystals. Whether this experiment was credible or not, remember everything is energy, everything is vibration. What you're thinking and feeling you are attracting.

The secret to attracting what you want in life is to be in tune with your thoughts, your feelings and your vibrations.

Principles of Feng Shui

Types of Teaching

The aim of using Feng Shui in our lives is to create simplicity and flow within our homes by allowing the space to be utilised for function as well as maximising positive energy to flow and bring good influences throughout the space we live in, giving a feeling of peace, harmony and fulfilment. Ultimately this leads to you becoming more productive and happier. There are four main types of Feng Shui teachings and each of them is beneficial in their own way. I'm going to explain the different types of teachings. There are no right or wrongs here and you can decide which aligns with you the best.

The Form

The first type is called "Form" Feng Shui. The Form system is the oldest documented type of Feng Shui, and is based on observing Chi through nature and land formations. The external surroundings of a home or structure are analysed to interpret the flow of energy. This would include things like waterways, mountains, or trees. Though rarely practiced by itself, you can find parts of the Form method still alive Today in combination with other styles of Feng Shui such as Flying Star Feng Shui. More commonly, these days it is combined with Compass methods as part of a traditional framework.

The Compass

The second type is the Compass Feng Shui. The Compass method was invented sometime after the age of Form. The Compass system of Feng Shui, it correlates to the points on a compass, North, South, East, West and in-between. Energies and symbols are connected to the eight directions of the compass and these are represented on a tool called the Magic Square, or Bagua. Use of a compass is always incorporated in this method. The compass is used to divide a home or business into eight sections that correspond to one of the five Chinese elements and a goal, such as wealth or career. Birth year and gender are used to determine one's Kua number. Kua numbers are a system of numerology based on your birth year and sex that is used in Feng Shui. Your Kua number is used to determine your favorable directions to face and locations for important areas of your home such as your front door and bedroom. Both the Form and the Compass classical methods are still practiced in Asia Today and have influenced modern Feng Shui in the Western world.

Flying Star Feng Shui

The third type is Flying Star Feng Shui. This form of Feng Shui uses Chinese astrology and the Chinese solar calendar to see how Chi flows over time and this is considered the most advanced form of science. Flying Star Feng Shui utilises the construction year of a dwelling and the eight directions of the compass to find patterns of Chi flow in the Bagua areas for the building or structure.

Black Hat Sect

The fourth and final type and more commonly used is the Black Hat Sect. In this book we will be focusing on this form which is a simplified form of Feng Shui, Black Hat Sect Feng Shui was brought to the West in 1986 by Thomas Lin Yun. Drawn from tenets of Tibetan Buddhism, it is also known as Western Feng Shui. This form of Feng Shui is extremely popular in Australia and the rest of the Western world, and is not based on the compass. Instead, the Bagua is mapped out using the entry door of each space. This form tends to depend on symbols, item placement, intention, and psychology. This form is more on the practical end, without being too spiritual.

Four Main Principles

These four main principles will help you map out, discover and create the best Chi in your home or work space. Before you begin, the aim is not to become a master at Feng Shui, but to take away valuable golden nuggets to help you transform your space and mind to become more productive and happier. When using Feng Shui you'll be able to arrange things to be spacious and clutter free, choose the right colours and decorative elements and use them in the specific areas of your home to bring about the best energy to your home or work, and to more importantly enhance the chosen areas of your life. You can, and should do this so that it compliments any existing decorative style inside your home and matches your personal taste. If you don't like how something looks, it'll be impossible to create positive energy around it. Therefore, Feng Shui is not a selection of strict rules, because no strictness brings a healthy flow of energy, which is what Feng Shui is all about. It is also not a simple practice of buying a bunch of Feng Shui symbols, such as wind chimes or crystals, and randomly placing them around your home. Feng Shui is about solving a problem. It's about understanding how things in our environment are related to one another and to ourselves and then taking the knowledge from this book that works for you and applying them to your space with thought and care.

1 Balance The Space

Balancing the space simply means to determine what the space will be used for. When you walk into a room you should have a sense of calm and brightness knowing everything has its purpose and place. Ensure your furniture lines like sofas, tables and cabinets are arranged in a way to create openness. Aim to provide good traffic patterns to make it easy to move around the room and choose the desired focal points. By doing this, furniture and items are placed in a way that creates good traffic flow which equals good energy flow and avoids walkways, rooms and spaces becoming obstructed by large items, sharp corners or clutter. This is an essential step to ensure each space is balanced evenly. The use of Yin and Yang will demonstrate how a balanced, peaceful space and mind is only achievable when there is harmony surrounding us. We will dive deeper into Yin and Yang within the next chapter.

2 The Five Elements

The five elements of Feng Shui are water, wood, fire, earth and metal. Their correct presence and placement in our space stimulates good Chi and promotes your well-being. Each element has its specific characteristics that will align with certain areas of your life. The optimal placement of the five elements is determined by the energy map of our space, called the B*agua* map in Feng Shui. The Bagua map tells us what part of our home needs which one of the five elements based on water, wood, fire, earth and metal. We will explore these elements in Chapter 4.

3 The Bagua Map

The Bagua map is a Feng Shui name for the energy map of your space. It shows which areas of your home are connected to which areas of your life. The black Hat Sec method of Feng Shui divides your space into nine areas including the centre. Each of these nine areas of your space, either your home or work place, corresponds to one of the five elements, which needs to be nourished in that area for good Feng Shui energy. So, say you'd like to enhance your self-worth through Feng Shui. You'd need to use the Bagua map to determine which area of your home is the self-worth area, and then use its corresponding element - wood, to stimulate the energy of that area. We will discover how to use this map in the next couple of chapters. Below is a diagram of the Bagua Map for the Black Hat Sec method.

WEALTH, PROSPERITY & SELF-WORTH WOOD PURPLE, GOLD	FAME, REPUTATION & SOCIAL LIFE FIRE RED, ORANGE	MARRIAGE AND RELATIONSHIPS EARTH PINK, SKIN AND EARTH TONES
HEALTH, FAMILY AND COMMUNITY WOOD GREEN, GOLD	GOOD FORTUNE CENTER EARTH YELLOW, EARTH TONES	CHILDREN, CREATIVITY AND FUN METAL WHITE, BRIGHT, PASTEL
WISDOM, & SELF-KNOWLEDGE EARTH BLUE, GREEN	CAREER, LIFE MISSION & INDIVIDUALITY WATER BLACK, DARK BLUES	HELP, CONTRIBUTION, SPIRIT AND TRAVEL METAL GRAYS, SILVER

4 Colour

It's no news that colour is an essential element in your home or space. But to understand how colour works in Feng Shui, we should remember that colour is the visual perception of light waves. Different wavelengths admit different colours. And since everything is energy including light, so is colour. We know by now that Feng Shui is all about energy. It's all about Chi and how it flows through your space. Different colours carry different energy qualities and symbolism, which are represented in the Bagua map and correspond to the energy of the five elements. Colour is probably the easiest way to quickly change the energy of a space, and since colour is tied to the specific elements, and the elements are tied to the Bagua areas, the application of colour will also depend on the nine areas of your space. To get a better idea of what colours represent and the areas and elements they align with, you can discover them in more detail using this chart provided.

COLOUR	ELEMENT	SYMBOLISUM	BAUGUA AREA	USE
WHITE	METAL	CLEANINESS, OPENESS AND PURITY	CREATIVITY, CONTRIBUTION AND TRAVEL	KITCHEN AND BEDROOMS
BLUE	WATER	SERENITY	MEDITATION, DEPENDABILITY AND CAREER	BEDROOMS AND BATHROOMS
BLACK	WATER	STRENTH, INDEPENDANCE AND MYSTICAL	KNOWLEDGE, CAREER AND POWER	BEDROOM FOR ADULTS OR TEENS
GREEN	WOOD	GROWTH AND HARMONY	FERTILITY, HEALTH AND FAMILY	BATHROOMS
YELLOW	EARTH	UPLIFTING, HAPPY AND SOCIAL	FAME, RELATIONSHIPS AND FREINDSHIPS	KITCHEN, LIVING AND DINING ROOM
RED	FIRE	STIMULATION	PASSION, FAME, PROSPERITY AND LOVE	ADULT BEDROOM, TONE/KITCHEN DINNING
ORANGE	FIRE	ACTIVE, CHEERFUL AND SOCIAL	FAME, ABUNDANCE AND REPUTATION	LIVING AND DINING ROOM
PINK	FIRE	HAPPINESS AND PURE THOUGHTS	LOVE AND ROMANCE	BEDROOM
PURPLE	WOOD	DIGNITY, GRACE, SPIRITUALITY AND SENSUALITY	CALMING, PROSPERITY, WEALTH AND LUCK	BEDROOMS, SHADES/LIVING ROOM
GOLD	METAL	PROSPERITY	WEALTH AND SPIRITUALITY	ACCENTS AND ACCESSORIES
GREY	METAL	NEUTRAL, CALM AND STILLNESS	KNOWLEDGE, CREATIVITY, CONTRIBUTION	UNDERTONE OR ACCENTS
BROWN	EARTH	GROUNDING AND MATERNAL	STABILITY AND CAREER	LIVING ROOM

Mastering Balance in Yin & Yang

Yin and Yang

Yin and Yang is a relational concept in Chinese culture that has developed over thousands of years. The meaning of Yin and Yang is that the universe is governed by a cosmic duality, two opposing and complementing principles or cosmic energies that can be observed in nature. In general, Yin is characterised as an inward energy that is feminine, still, dark, and negative. On the other hand, Yang is characterised as outward energy, masculine, hot, bright, and positive. Yin and Yang are not two separate energies, but two halves of the same whole which equal Chi. Positive Chi that brings happiness and good fortune to a space is made up of both Yin and Yang. The constant movement and interplay of these two forces results in one always trying to outdo the other. Balance is what you're looking for in a Feng Shui environment. Yin and Yang can be found in everything. When you examine the space you are in, you should be able to pinpoint where there is too much Yin or too much Yang. The flow and feel of the energy will tell you, however you can use this chart below as a guide. Example: Yin energy is low key, and can be found in bathrooms and bedrooms as these are places that should be very calm and relaxing. Yang energy is more active and may more often be felt in the kitchen, living room, or family room. Imagine if every day of your life was in darkness. Would that feel balanced? Or picture living somewhere where there was only heat, sunlight, but no water or anything else to provide some coolness. The same applies to your mindset. Yin energy creates a state of peace and contentment, while Yang energy creates a state of liveliness and emotion. Picture spending each day with no emotional excitement, would you feel balanced? Or experiencing every day feeling on edge or anxious. Yin and Yang demonstrates how a balanced, peaceful space and mind is only achievable when there is harmony surrounding us.

The diagram provided explains the differences between Yin and Yang. Once you get the hang of it, it will become easier to distinguish the balance in an existing space.

Feminine - Moon - Darkness - Depression

Dull Colours - Blues - Greys - Slow Moving

Cold - Stillness - Passive/Repetitive

Earthly - Soft - Odd Numbers

Sleep - Inside – Down

Masculine - Sun - Bright - Active

Bright Colours - Reds - Orange - Fast Moving

Hit - Movement - Active

Heavenly - Hard - Even Numbers

Awake - Outside - Up

The Five Elements of Space

The five elements correspond to five different energy types, these work together in a supportive movement. The elements are water, wood, fire, earth and metal. Elements can help, weaken, create, or cause bad vibes when they interact with one another. But collectively these elements represent various aspects of Chi, each having positive and negative attributes within themselves. These elements are present in people and in things.

Knowing what areas you want to focus on in the nine areas of life, will help you decide what elements you should focus on within the space you reside in.

Water

The water element symbolises emotions, beauty and art. It may also symbolise stress by draining Yin. This element serves people who are communicators, intuitive, social and artistic as well as people who can be sensitive and indecisive. Things that correspond to this elements are, bodies of water, pictures of water (ensure they are in motion), glass, mirrors, fountains, fish tanks and primary colours of blue and black.

Wood

The wood element symbolises growth, stableness and vast nurturing. It may also symbolise flexibility. This element serves people who are idealist, starters, social and artistic. It also serves the entrepreneurial mindset which goes hand in hand with people who can be a little impatient. Things that correspond to this element are trees, landscapes, plants or anything that is basically made of wood. The primary colour being green and brown.

Fire

The fire element symbolises heat, light and warmth. It may also symbolise destruction, honour and aggression in Yang. This element serves people who are leaders, ambitious and inspiring. It also serves people who are seeking action and innovation. Things that correspond to this element are the sun, fireplaces, triangular shapes, candles and lights. The primary colour is red.

Earth

The earth element symbolises support, growth and nurturing. It may also symbolise fairness and concern. This element serves people who are loyal, supportive and patient. It also serves people who are dependable, practical and fussy. Things that correspond with this element are rocks, clay, cement stone and brick. The primary colours are yellow, orange and brown. Central to Feng Shui is also the earth element, which brings unity, peace and harmony to an entire space. An overall sense of peace, good luck, and grounding can be felt in relationships, in the family, and in the structure itself when the earth element is balanced. Symbols of earth include crystals and ceramics. Be mindful of keeping too much of the wood or metal element near your earth element as they both work against earth's energy.

Metal

The metal element symbolises strength, fortitude and communication. It may also symbolise sadness and danger. The element serves people who are assertive, focused and organised. It also serves people who are independent, intuitive and stubborn. Things that correspond to this element are metals, round objects like coins, metal weapons and ornaments. The primary colours are white, silver and gold. While metal is strongly associated with gold, silver, and wealth, the element is also connected to lifestyle. Work carefully with elements of metal to help attract income or wealth and avoid the coldness.

Using The Five Elements

Learning these correspondences teaches you how to use the elements in your home or work place. For example, fire is an energiser, the energy can be harnessed through the use of candles or lights. Water can energise or de-energise, depending on how it's used.

Placing water (or its symbols, such as the colour blue) in the opposite area to fire, can help attract wealth energy. Water elements can also be used to temper the energy and psychology. For example a picture of a sinking ship in your office isn't going to serve you any favours in business. Combinations of elements can work well together, for example: Wood symbolises strength and growth and can work together with water in certain spaces. Plants fall under the element of wood, and may be used to hide flaws in a structure or act as a boost for success in a space. So, say you would like to enhance your relationship through Feng Shui. You would need to use the Bagua map to determine which area of your home is the relationship area, and then use its corresponding elements to stimulate the energy of that area. This may mean removing family pictures out of the bedroom space and introducing more romance with colour like purples and pinks.

Correspondences are a guide to how the elements are expressed in a room. Use of colour, shape, or material forms is at your control to enhance or tune an area. Having too much of any element represented in a home our work space can affect good Chi. When working with elements, you want to make sure you understand how they relate to one another and how you combine them together to make a difference. Knowing that the purpose of a room will also point you in the direction of what energy should support it.

The Nine Life Areas

How do you manage everything in your life? How do you find the balance? Remind yourself not to get overwhelmed with it all. The aim is not to try and control every area of your life, but to enhance the areas you value the most. For example, if health and fitness is on your top priorities, then you most likely hold value in this area. If you are struggling with your finances, you may want to evaluate your values on wealth and use this as an area to focus on. We are going to dive into the nine life areas and you will gain an idea of what you need to focus on to achieve fulfillment, peace and harmony.

Career/Life Mission/Individuality

This area resides in the element of moving water. One of the most important, yet one of the most neglected areas of life. Do you remember being asked the question "what do you want to do, once you grow up"? You only just realised that as a young teen/adult you start to weigh up options. Do you study further to higher education and possibly become a teacher, accountant or a lawyer, or learn a trade to have work for years to come. What if you could ask yourself a different question... "Who do you want to be" instead of "What do you want to do". "Do" has a different meaning to "Be". As human beings we are being not doing. You see there's a difference, and when you understand this difference you realise that in life your individuality is everything, it creates purpose and without this purpose or mission there will come a point where you will feel unfulfilled, unmotivated, questioning the path you have taken has anything to do with who you really want to be. The good news is that you can create a new career, a new life mission and become the person you want to be at any point in time. You just have to ask yourself the right question. Working on your passion → You are in tune with your purpose → Purpose sparks desire → Desire ignites motivation.

Health/Family/Community

This area resides in the element of wood. An area that many people value strongly. Health is such a broad term. When we think of health, we think of our physical body, our nutrition and exercise. However health is contributed by physical and mental elements. It is also highly affected by the people in and around your life. You may not know it, but your family, friends, your neighbours and community play a huge effect on the way you feel, the way you think and the way you live your life. It is said "You become the average of the five people you associate with the most". Think about this for a second. List up the five closest people in your life right now. Are they lighting up your fire or are they dampening your flame? To create ultimate health, you'll need the right ingredients. Fuel your body with good nutrition, exercise regularly, surround yourself with people who are kind, compassionate and only want the best for you and most importantly, cut out the people who aren't building you up. Sounds harsh, but trust me, you will thank yourself for it later. What if the problem is a family member or close friend? Obviously don't cut them off completely, that's not an option for most, but just spend less time with them so they are not in your top five. Choose wisely, people you surround yourself with will influence you and your health more than you'll ever know.

Children/Creativity/Fun

This area resides in the element of metal. Our brain is wired to be creative. Creation is something that can't be forced nor triggered at will. It can and will appear when you least expect it. Creation is simply a collection of exposures, experiences or moments gathered into your thoughts. At any time these can be simultaneously linked together to create something new. The secret to being creative is to expose yourself to things that influence your thoughts, to get out and meet people, enjoy new experiences and most importantly, have fun and find that inner child. The emotion of joy has a high frequency of Chi and together this will help you attract inspiration and creation.

Fame/Reputation/Social

This area resides in the element of fire. Fame and reputation are the foundations of our personal journey. They develop and change over time and can be affected in a positive or negative way. Fame can change a person, you see this all over the media with famous actors and actresses, from musicians to politicians. Did you know, some of the wealthiest people live amongst us unknown and out of the spotlight. Whether you are living your life in the opinion of others or whether you are living your life for yourself, your reputation plays an important part in how people see you and how you see yourself. Think about the people you like to follow or learn from. Are they kind, compassionate, and thoughtful? Are they good listeners, integral and loyal? These are just some of the qualities that will help you earn a good reputation.

Have you ever heard of "The Four Agreements"? Below are some golden nuggets from the book to help you in the area of life relating to our social interactions.

Agreement 1: "Be impeccable with your words".

Your word is the most powerful tool at your disposal for creating things. But it's a double-edged sword: with your word you can create the most beautiful dream, or can destroy everything around you. The human mind is like a fertile ground where seeds are continually being planted. The seeds are planted with words (ideas, opinions, concepts) – if you plant bad seeds with bad words, you're going to get rotten fruit. It's important to recognise that your 'word' is not just the things you say out loud to other people, but also the things you say to yourself in your own head.

Agreement 2: "Don't take anything personally".

Imagine someone walks up to you in the street and says, "you're stupid". Hopefully you don't give this person's opinion any weight and you go about your day unaffected, but it's easy to get dragged down by what people around us say. You will realise that most comments and thoughts and opinions of others say a lot more about them than they do about us. If your boss lashes out and says your work isn't up to scratch, maybe she or he has just been having a rough week. If the barista at the cafe doesn't smile at you, maybe they just got verbally abused by an irritated customer and they haven't fully recovered yet. In any scenario like this, recognise that these aren't meant personally for us. Therefore, we can try to move past them with kindness and compassion.

Agreement 3: "Don't make assumptions".

Making assumptions is really asking for problems. How it works is that you take a tiny piece of information then extrapolate it to paint a full picture. If you believe that this picture you've painted (based on one small piece of information) gives you a firm grasp of the situation then you're doomed for disaster. Your assumptions can easily be a byproduct of your experience or your current emotional state.

The way to combat guessing, is to have the courage to admit that you don't know, and always ask questions. By gathering information, you can truly know something rather than just assuming.

Agreement 4: "Always do your best".

It seems obvious, but are you truly doing your best whenever you can? I'm sure you had times in your life when you did your best and times when you could've done better. It could've been something big or small, like a daily interaction with someone, the way you spoke with your children or served customers at work. If you don't do your best there is a gap between how you perform and how you know that you could perform if you tried your best. You may try to fill this gap with guilt or regret for not doing the best you possibly could have. If every moment in your life you do your best, then there is no room for regret in your life. And if one day you don't do your best? Don't stress about it, don't worry about it, don't replay the moment over and over in your head. Put a full stop at the end of that day. Tomorrow is another opportunity for you to do your best. For a deeper understanding of these rules I would highly recommend you dive into this book "The Four Agreements" by Don Miguel Ruiz.

Wisdom/Knowledge/Rest

This area resides in the element of earth. Towards wisdom there's a long way to go, you may think. To become wise, the first step is information, but here's the catch… There is so much information out there and you could spend days researching information, filling your mind with endless amounts of clutter. Information is actually useless if it's not used! Letting go of information that does not serve your mission, goal or life right now allows room for you to learn new things. It's like an old martial arts saying, you can't fill up your cup of knowledge if your existing cup is already half full. Using the information we acquire such as a skill we have learnt and putting that skill into practice creates knowledge. Knowledge is the experience from the practice of the information… see where we are going here? Now, to become wise, this is based on experience + time + failure + success. It's knowing about the challenges and how to overcome them. To gain real wisdom, choose something you wish to learn, gather the information, practice and master this skill. To truly master a skill you must become obsessed with it.

Wealth/Prosperity/Self-Worth

This area resides in the element of wood. Wealth is a collective area of life, which includes time, money, health and your whole overall wellbeing. Prosperity is when you are living an example of this ideal life that you have created, living in peace, harmony and in a carefree manner. Very few people manage to achieve this level of wealth and prosperity, it's an art that must be practiced each day. One of the key factors to achieving this abundance of wealth is having self-worth. What is self-worth? When fear does not affect your decisions, where self-doubt is just a concept and your belief in yourself and your values is more powerful than anyone's opinion. Self-worth is the value you place on yourself. If you have a high level of self-worth, you will view yourself as unstoppable and have pure faith that you can set and achieve your goals in life. Even with difficulties and challenges in the way, you will tell yourself (and genuinely believe it!) - that you deserve all things good. Having self-worth is also linked to having a strong sense of confidence, a strong posture and a solid projection. As a fitness coach I came across with key principles for achieving goals no different to any other goal in life. The ones that succeeded had self-worth and the ones that failed had little to none. Building this confidence comes with patience, practice and determination. If you want to achieve it, you need to believe you can achieve it. Discipline will not always serve you until the end, however your self respect will. Whatever you want in life, remind yourself, you deserve it.

Marriage/Relationships/Partners

This area resides in the element of earth. I dare to say that this is on the top of the most important areas of life. Whether you are married, have a partner or single with your best friend being a dog or cat. This area could gain importance to you at some stage. The bond you share with one another is one that requires consistent communication and energy, this area needs energy. Giving your energy is the key to a successful relationship. What I mean by this is to be present, communicate, discuss life in its happiest and darkest hours and if there are problems, do whatever it takes to solve them together. This brings me to the subject of love. Love for your partner, family or friends. Love is not a word, love is an action based on love and trust. It's about the things you do for each other each day, the support through the good and bad times. It's about listening and seeking to understand before being understood. Relationships are the foundation of success. Behind every successful person there is a supporter, an influencer, a believer in you and your personal mission and if this area is important to you, you will agree to that. Love is the most powerful emotion. It is said that life is fulfilled if one has loved and been loved.

Contribution/Travel/Spiritual

This area resides in the element of metal. Contribution is a natural coding within us. You are wired to serve others because in some strange way making someone else genuinely happy, makes you happy. Watching someone open a present bought by you or helping a person jumpstart their car on the side of the road for most, will genuinely stratify our spirit and karma. Giving something to see it succeed can be one of the most rewarding feelings. Another way to enhance this area of life is to travel. When you are "well travelled" you are exposed to different ways of life, smells, sights and cultures. Not only does this contribute to your happiness, it gives you a different perspective on life, it shifts the paradigm and broadens your view on how others live life. It also enlightens your spiritual connection to others and gives you a deeper meaning to life. Travel is good for the soul.

Good Fortune/Centre

This area resides in the element of earth. The centre of good fortune is the combination of all life's areas. It is said that Good Fortune signifies luck. The fact is, luck doesn't exist, it's a concept. What does exist is attraction. What you think about you can manifest. To be "lucky" is a conscious projection of energy and Chi. Whenever you focus and work on an area of life to become successful, the results of your thoughts and actions assist you to thrive in that area. The centre is the result of what you have projected out, to what you have reflected straight into your life. It is a collective area of thoughts and manifestation throughout the mind and space you live in. It is the area - when fulfilled - that will provide you with the feeling of peace and harmony. It wasn't luck of the draw, it was all you. You have the true power to establish how your life unfolds and in which direction.

PART II

Curing The Chaos

It's now time to put this power into practice by using these principles of Feng Shui. By following this process, you'll be set for success and will learn how to create a positive and influential space to help you become more productive and happier.

Clear the Clutter

It is in human nature to accumulate things that no longer play a specific function in the home. Clutter is not just unpleasant to see, it's an energy drainer that prevents the best things from unfolding in your life. An excessive amount of clutter will stop you from having clarity of thoughts and can weigh you down emotionally. Feng Shui isn't about having a perfectly-styled home, it's more about creating a happy and healthy environment. When everything has its place, it's easy to stay organised.

I used to think the best way to start was to clear clutter by room. I would take on the garage first, then the kitchen, then the office next. Instead, what works best is to start tidying by category. Begin with clothing, as clothing is one of the least emotionally attaching materials. With your eyes now open, you may now realise your wardrobe has hit rock bottom. It's a mixed up madness and once you declutter, it's time to get organised. One way to help this overwhelming choice of where you keep and place certain items is to consider your clothing's feelings: Yeh, they don't technically have feelings, but remember what you just learned: Everything is vibration, everything is energy. So let's ask ourselves, if clothes did have feelings, are they happy being squashed in a corner shelf, or crowded onto hangers? Are your hardworking shoes really thrilled to be boxed up or tossed on the porch? When you think this way you may start to identify that your clothes are really looking miserable and a change needs to happen for your wardrobe to feel peaceful and harmonised. It's important not to be distracted. Only focus on the category you are organising. To begin, place all your items from the category in the middle of the room. All your items, every single of them. Pick up each individual item and ask yourself if it still sparks you joy? This question of joy gives you permission to let go of everything that fulfilled its purpose. Once this task is done correctly, you will feel relieved and lighter. It will also feel like good karma when your things are sold or donated to a charity store, off to spark joy for someone else.

Once you've sorted out the things to discard—and only then—you can decide where the remaining things should go. Rather than folded in a cupboard or hanging in a wardrobe, clothing for example looks happier folded in a chest of drawers or tallboy. I used to hang 80% of my clothing, but now, having begun with a large overflowing wardrobe, I was down to enough clothing to fill one wardrobe and one drawer.

Tops, pants, and shirts now destined for the drawers. Vertical folding technique makes everything easy to spot and hard to mess up (you aren't disrupting a whole pile every time you take something out or put something back). Folded this way, clothing looks like fabric origami, aiming to line your drawers in neat rows. Also while you are folding by hand, you and the fabric make continuous contact of energy and an exchange of Chi. To keep these little folded packages standing at attention in the drawers, I would suggest using shoe boxes as drawer dividers.

Once you've cleared away the clutter and put things away, your clothes and clothing accessories can see the light of day. There's breathing room between pieces, so you no longer have to do that awkward arm wrestle with the racks. All of which means you get a sense of joy when you are entering the space by just opening your wardrobe. Whether you're getting ready in the morning or planning a night out, it will feel easier to find things that define your style.

This method is known worldwide as the KonMari method by the amazing organising expert Marie Kondo. It can be applied to any category including your kitchen, living room, garage or office. Follow these simple rules and you'll be clutter free, stress free and able to define your new style. For more information on the KonMari method I would recommend her book "Spark Joy".

Positive Flow

The layout of your space determines the flow of energy in a room. Let's talk about furniture and flow. Positive flow is the traffic flow of Chi within your home or work space. The aim is to create traffic patterns to enable the perfect amount of good energy to enter your home and move around freely with this space also being fully functional for purpose.

This refers back to "balancing the space". Balancing the space simply means to determine what the space will be used for. Ensure your lines, traffic patterns and desired focal points are arranged in balance so furniture and items are placed in a way that creates good traffic flow, easy energy flow and avoids walkways, rooms and spaces becoming obstructed by large items, sharp corners or clutter. To do this, start by designing a floor plan. Set the intention for the function of the room. Decide on a main focal point, which could be a fireplace, wall mural behind a bed or a garden water feature. Select the furniture you wish to keep and which you need to remove. You may even need additional items to balance the weight in the room. Work with your existing furniture first and then make the changes required to suit. Each room is individual to your taste, however it's a good idea to use the Bagua map to guide you in the best elements and colours for your furniture, walls and floors. A copy of this map is located in the back of this book. When the arrangement of a room is done correctly, not only will it improve the functionality, it will improve the energy of the space and promote a more positive feeling of balance and harmony. Here are a few tips to help you achieve positive flow.

1: Slow The Chi

When you invite a visitor into your home, it would be weird for them to head straight to the bedroom or kitchen, right? Well, I know a few that would head straight to the kitchen! Jokes aside, you want them to linger in the common area. This is no different when it comes to the movement of Chi. When there is a direct line-of-sight between the front door and the back door, it means the Chi is racing through the house too fast. Instead of having it fly straight out the back door, you must try to navigate it gracefully, so that it goes around your whole home evenly to balance an equal amount of energy in each area. Slow-up the energy flowing into your home or work space by adding a feature or artwork that causes you to pause and reflect without blocking or affecting traffic flow. The entrance to your home or work space has the biggest impact on the Chi, as it's where the main amount of energy enters. A set of French doors or glass partitions are a good way to slow this energy down, or if this isn't an option, a detailed rug or art work can divert the attention from the rear of the space and steady the Chi. The biggest mistake is the use of a mirror directly reflecting the front door. This mirror would act as a deflection for any Chi trying to enter your home. Instead, ensure mirrors are hung effectively in a position that reflects energy into an area or reflects an existing feature.

2: Use The Five Elements

The five elements, water, wood, fire, earth and metal can be present in your home either physically or symbolically. For example, you could bring the fire element with warm tones, like reds and oranges or you could have actual fire with a fireplace or a burning candle. Look closely at the physical and symbolic elements that are showing up in your home, as they can be a cause of imbalance in your emotional life. The aim is to create balance between all elements. You will discover this more in chapter eight - "Elements and Energy".

3: Remove Negative Symbols

If you look closely, symbols are constantly affecting you on an everyday basis. From news, to radio, to road signs, we're always being guided by symbols. In our homes, it's enhanced even more, because we are creating intimate environments that most often represent our fears and challenges and views based on our own experiences. Often we can unknowingly reinforce these challenges in our lives by allowing what we constantly see in our space to take an effect. Do you have trouble getting clarity? Check if you have stuff all over your surfaces. Do you have self-worth issues? Check if your mirrors are hung too high, so you can never measure up. Are you always single? Assess if you're loading up your home with single imagery—a single vase, a single candle, a single person in a picture. Evaluate what challenges you are facing in life and try to identify whether they're reflecting in your space. Remove the symbols and replace them with items you want to project out so that you can attract that straight back into your life.

4: Light It Up

It's no surprise that lighting can affect our mood and more so natural light can make us feel happier and more positive. Mirrors in Feng Shui are like drugs, they're prescribed often to treat many ailments. They're a quick adjustment when you want to expand a space and bring in more light. The key is to be very mindful of what the mirrors reflect. Is it a beautiful view or a blank wall, is it reflecting Chi or blocking the energy from entering your home. When you hang a mirror, make sure it reflects more light, a serene view, or an expansive part of the room.

Elements & Energy

It's time to dive a little deeper into the world of elements and energy. Just like we discovered in the previous chapter "The Five Elements Of Space", these elements correspond to five different energy types and they work together in a supportive movement. Water serves wood to grow like trees and plants, wood serves fire to burn like the wood in a fireplace, fire serves the earth with its leftover ashes and the earth creates precious metals by compounding chemical reactions in the rocks like the way iron ore is formed. Let's say your kitchen is set up with the cooker on one side and the sink on the other. Every kitchen has an element of heat and water, and these elements have a negative effect on each other. Fire destroys water, and water destroys fire. So how do we fix this? One way to complement these elements, is to place an element of wood in-between, this could be a plant or wooden decorative symbols. This would allow all three elements to harmonise. Once you get your head around it, it's going to become a lot easier to discover. Take a look at this chart provided to see how each element can have a positive or negative effect on each other.

Element	Creates	Weakens	Destroys
FIRE	EARTH	WOOD	METAL
EARTH	METAL	FIRE	WATER
METAL	WATER	EARTH	WOOD
WATER	WOOD	METAL	FIRE
WOOD	FIRE	WATER	EARTH

"Energy is Chi. A vital force that completely surrounds you and the environment. Chi is universal, it surrounds you and makes up everything in the universe. Chi resides within each element and the energy must be balanced between Yin and Yang".

Balance is what you're looking for in a Feng Shui environment. Yin and Yang can be found in these elements shown in the chart below.

Element	Energy	Yin Or Yang
WATER	Adaptation - Flow	Yin
EARTH	Softness - Purity - Growth	Yin
WOOD	Dark - Bold - Thunder	Yang
WOOD	Light - Flowing - Serene	Yin
EARTH	Centre of Collective Energy	
METAL	Strong - Heavy - Hevenly - Unbendable	Yang
METAL	Soft - Flexible - Reflection	Yin
EARTH	Strong - Solid - Scenic - Mountains	Yang
FIRE	Smart - Impulsive - Energetic	Yang

"Yin is characterised as an inward energy that is feminine, still, dark and negative. Yang is characterised as outward energy, masculine, hot, bright and positive. Yin and Yang are not two separate energies, but two halves of the same whole which equal Chi".

How do these elements represent themselves in Yin and Yang? Water represents the energy of Yin. It flows effortlessly and it is most suited situated at the opposite end of your home to Fire. For example if you have a fireplace in the front room of your home then a water feature would be placed at the rear. In other teachings of Feng Shui, a compass is used to determine the position of your element, however we are going to focus on the Black Hat Sec method using the psychological effects to suit every space you reside in. Earth represents the energy of Yin with softness and the element of Yang with solid mountains or rocks. Wood represents the energy of Yin with things like wooden wind chimes and light tones of colour. It represents the energy of Yang with solid heavy woods and dark bold tones of colour. Metal represents the energy of Yin with soft flexible materials and light reflections. Strong heavy metals that are unbendable represent Yang. Fire ultimately is the energy of Yang and opposite to water. Now you're getting the hang of it and hopefully starting to understand how elements play an important part in creating peace, balance and harmony within your home or work space. You will now begin to understand the power of the elements and their meaning, the importance of balance between Yin and Yang together with the combination of the Bagua map to determine your chosen area to enhance within the nine life areas.

Psychological Symbols

As you have read in the previous chapters, symbols are constantly affecting you on an everyday basis. They often represent our fears and challenges and should be used to represent our goals and achievements. By allowing what we constantly see in our space to have a positive effect, we can create psychological influences to help build us up.

Psychological Symbols - Chinese Deities

Chinese deities are often included as remedies to enhance the amount of positive Chi in a space. They can provide protection or attract wealth, good health and good fortune. They can be found in a statue or picture form and placed around your home or business to release powerful influence. Here are just a few examples:

The Three Star Gods – Fuk, Luk, and Sau – Fuk represents prosperity and happiness; Luk, prosperity and authority, and Sau, health and longevity. Luk is always placed in the centre, with Fuk to his right and Sau to his left.

Kuan Kung – As a guardian, Kuan Kung offers protection, prosperity and harmony. He should face the front entrance.

Laughing Buddha – With his round belly, Laughing Buddha gives a boost to Chi and brings wealth, cheer, health and good fortune to the home. His placement in various sectors of a space improves luck, ability to meet goals, harmony in families and material gain.

Kwan Yin – Kwan Yin is the goddess of compassion, mercy, forgiveness and love. She is a protector and looks after those who are suffering. She can help get rid of negative energy at home, work or a business.

Plant and Flower Symbols

Live flowers and plants can be used to bring good Chi into a space, just as can art and other decorative accents. Though they represent the wood element, plants can also balance fire and water elements in the kitchen. If live plants are not preferred, artificial plants can work. You can also easily locate some of these items as framed art:

- **Bamboo**: thriving plant that symbolises luck, strength
- **Lotus**: immortality, prosperity, endurance, enlightenment
- **Jade Plant**: powerful for wealth, prosperity

- **Citrus Trees**: health, prosperity good fortune; can be bought as miniature versions or artificial trees

- **Money Plant**: called "the Feng Shui plant"; represents luck, fortune, income, wealth, metal element

- **Peony**: relationships, romance, true love

- **Chrysanthemum**: happiness, optimism, energising

- **Plum Blossoms**: fragrant flower that brings good fortune

- **Narcissus**: wealth prosperity, career growth

- **Peace Lily**: luck, peace, harmony

- **Cherry Blossoms**: promote marital harmony, youthfulness

- **Geranium**: fire element

Food Symbols

In Feng Shui, fruit is connected to nature and therefore the Chi energy. Each fruit carries a specific energetic aspect of Chi and having them in the space will attract that energy type. Having fresh bowls of fruit will attract positive Chi. Fruit art works serve well also. Certain foods and plants were inaccessible to people in ancient China due to the cost, so pictures and other pieces of art served as substitutes. Therefore fresh fruit or art that has fruit in it can be used as an option.

- **Peach**: symbol of immortality, heaven, health, wealth, prosperity, love, marital bliss

- **Pomegranate**: fertility, luck, happiness

- **Orange**: wards off bad luck, purifies, 9 oranges kept together in the kitchen or living room attract good luck

- **Pineapple**: good fortune, luck, abundance

- **Apple**: luck, peace, harmony

Crystals

Crystals are used frequently in Feng Shui as cures for spaces and one's personal life areas. Now I'm not suggesting magic crystals work, however if it contributes to helping you trigger a good state of mind then I'm all for the magic crystals. It's said that each crystal carries a specific vibration that is used to enhance a different area.

- **Clear Quartz**: attracts clean Chi to an area, energises

- **Rose Quartz**: love, peace, compassion, forgiveness

- **Jade**: balances the emotions, brings peace, luck, happiness, abundance

- **Black Tourmaline**: protection; dispels negativity, anxiety, anger

- **Amber:** healing, fights illness

- **Amethyst:** calming, helps with insomnia, reduces stress, promotes strength, spiritual, transforms negative Chi into positive Chi

- **Kyanite**: loyalty, good communication, success in business or career

- **Hematite**: grounding

- **Citrine**: creativity, abundance

- **Moonstone**: creativity

- **Tiger's Eye**: protection, earth element

Prosperity Symbols and Chi Enhancers

- **Gold Ingots** – Auspicious symbol of good luck and wealth. Ingots were once a form of gold currency. They are typically placed in wealth vases, or areas of the home or business where financial and wealth Chi needs to be activated. They should not be placed too close to fire element symbols.

- **Ru Yi Scepter** – A symbol of power, authority, and status. Wonderful for managers or those who are ambitious.

- **Emperor Coins** – Wealth enhancements that originate from the Ching Dynasty. Place in the wealth sector, wealth vases or with other wealth figures.

- **Fortune Flower Coins** – Feature engravings that draw blessings for every Feng Shui area, including health, success, wealth and protection.

- **Lucky Coins** – Seen tied together with red strings. They represent wealth blessings and help attract good fortune while deflecting negative Chi. Found in businesses and homes.

- **Five Element Pagoda** – Powerful. Absorbs negative Chi. Each level represents an element: earth-metal-water-wood-fire.

- **Feng Shui Crystal Balls** – Clear crystals that get rid of bad Chi, restore positive Chi, and can cleanse a space.

- **Crystal Spheres** – Round crystal globes that bring calmness, harmony, and peace to an environment. Can break up arguments, chaos, competition, and discontent in homes and offices. Often used in groups of 6. They can be found made of clear quartz, amethyst, rose quartz, obsidian and other materials.

- **Wu Lou** – The gourd. It presents blessings of good health and longevity and can absorb negative Chi in a space.

- **Sailing Ships** – Symbolises wealth sailing into the business or home. Increases income, opportunities and material gain. Must make sure the ship is facing inwards towards the direction of Chi entering your space.

Wind Chimes

Wind chimes are a classic remedy in Feng Shui; their sound increases the flow of positive Chi in an environment. Depending on which element (metal, earth, etc.) they are made of, they can also suppress energies. Wind chimes are typically made of metal, ceramic, glass, wood or bamboo. When selecting a set, look for those made of one uniform material, versus a combination. Chimes should have a clear sound when rung.

The bagua denotes which type of wind chime material is best to use for each sector of the home, according to the five elements. Metal chimes are for the areas of children, creativity, fun, travel and spirituality. Wood and bamboo wind chimes go well in the areas of wealth, prosperity, self-worth, health, family and community, while ceramic or glass chimes are placed in the areas representing wisdom and self-knowledge or relationships.

Avoid hanging wind chimes directly above a bed, eating area, workspace or where people stand for periods of time - it creates negative Chi. If there's not enough wind to make them ring indoors, ring them by hand each day.

Each part of a home or space should have a common thread running through it. Whether it's through colour, art or another element, there should be something connecting family members to one another and their environment. An example would be a house where the parents are both musicians. Instruments and music memorabilia are found throughout the space, except in the child's room, where there are none. To make a connection, adding a music related item or an instrument in the child's bedroom would establish that link. Further, pieces of that child's identity and interests should of course also be used to furnish and decorate his or her room.

As you can now see, symbols are an important part of the psychological benefits to help enhance the positive Chi in your home or work space. Whatever area of life you choose to grow and develop, choose your visual influences wisely and allow the abundance and manifestation to flow into your life.

PART III

Seven Daily Practices To Own Your Day

Now that you have gained an understanding on how to adapt your way of thinking and harmonise the space around you. Feng Shui alone will not help you create the life you desire without practicing positive daily habits. You are about to learn seven essential daily practices to help you live life around the chaos with a more positive, productive and happy environment, for a life of greater peace and harmony.

I.

Start With Sleep

Getting a good night's sleep is the key to starting the day right. Sleeping enables you to recharge your body and cultivate Chi. There is a mountain of research out there that suggests the average person requires six to seven hours of good sleep each night. In Today's fast-paced society, six or seven hours of sleep may sound pretty good. In reality, depending on what you do during your working day, what may be a recipe for sleep deprivation. You may feel that you're able to function well operating on five or six hours of sleep; however, if you spent an extra hour in bed, would you feel more energised and efficient? With all the information out there regarding sleep, the common conclusions suggest that sleeping less than six hours or having continuous broken sleep will affect your concentration, clarity, energy and mood, so ensuring you get between seven and nine hours should be an essential goal for most. There's also a flip side to this, oversleeping! Too much sleep on a regular basis can increase the risk of diabetes, heart disease, stroke and even death according to several studies done over the years. Too much is defined as more than nine hours. The most common cause is not getting enough sleep the night before or cumulatively during the week. You may also have experienced that it's not always easy to have continuous nights of harmonious, deep, relaxing sleep. In the real world you are likely to be surrounded by a noisy neighbour, cat fights or road noise. You may have children that keep you up at night or you go to bed with a thousand thoughts, worries and concerns. So how do we create habits to ensure we can gain optimal sleep? Here are my successful practices you can choose to implement that will help you to enhance the best night's sleep ever.

1: Eat Dinner Early.

When you eat dinner your body processes the carbohydrates, proteins and fats - we call these macronutrients. This typically happens while you are still awake and active. If you go to bed with a full stomach, it may affect how you sleep, as the digestive fluids and acids in your stomach are active while you are processing the food you just ate. When you lie down to sleep after eating, your whole body is in a horizontal position which could lead to you feeling heartburn, acid reflux, and indigestion. Your metabolism slows as your body prepares for rest so you don't typically need the additional calories. If you're hungry, aim for a healthy snack before bed or light dinner at least two - three hours before you hit the pillow. A big breakfast and smaller dinners are the way to go, benefiting you with better digestion and better sleep, taking into account your total daily requirement in calories for each day.

2: Avoid alcohol

There's nothing wrong with a glass of wine in an evening, however understanding that alcohol is a carbohydrate which requires digestion enables you to decide if you need that extra stomach activity before you sleep. Although you may think a couple of beverages will help you sleep, it's actually the opposite. The reason you may experience a lack of sleep after a few vinos is not only the digestion of empty calories, but you'll find yourself becoming dehydrated during the night which ultimately disrupts your sleep. Staying hydrated is an important ingredient for sleep. If you're going to kick back with a glass of red in the evening, ensure you stop early and drink a glass of water before bed. Use the bathroom before sleep so that you're not getting up and interrupting sleep.

3: Ditch The Screens

You've most likely heard this before, but there are valid reasons to turn off the screens before sleep. iPads, phones, Tv screens all contain a blue light which is known to suppress melatonin levels. Suppressed production of melatonin makes it difficult for you to "switch off" your brain and fall asleep. You may also be filling up your thoughts with news or ideas stimulating more emotions and energy. Rule of thumb, turn off screens 30-60 minutes before sleep time.

4: Tea Before Bed

After drinking a warm cup of tea, you'll feel ready for bedtime. It's important to choose a tea that is free of sleep-disrupting caffeine. You should also avoid adding sugar to your tea before bedtime, since the sugar may increase energy and digestion. Tea can be used with silent meditation, as you focus on the tea and yourself. As you drink tea, you also meditate and submerge yourself in the calmness and stillness. It's a great way to take a break from your busy life and to relax while staying hydrated before sleep.

5: Brain Dump

Brain dumping is simply off loading all your thoughts and ideas. You can do this as many times a day as you need and use multiple methods to do so. The classic way of this is the use of notepads. By dumping all your thoughts for the day onto paper, you are letting go of the chaos within your mind, freeing up precious storage and releasing some of that mental tension. Just as the benefits of decluttering your space, a brain dump is a simple technique to help you declutter your mind and thoughts. It helps you gain focus on things that need doing. Brain dumping also helps you organise your time and efforts, meaning you basically become more productive and calmer. One of the most fundamental practices for successful people is to organise thoughts into "To Do" lists. Another great way is the use of mind-mapping. This is where you can actually see a clear map of your thoughts and tasks. You can download many free Apps, one I recommend for Mac is "MindNode".

6: Meditate

How do we understand meditation? Meditation is about training awareness and getting a healthy sense of perspective. You're not trying to turn off your thoughts or feelings. You're just learning to observe them without judgment. As you become aware, you become mindful, which gives you the ability to be present, to rest in the here and now, fully engaged with whatever you are doing in the moment. Meditation is like learning any other skill, it's like training that muscle that you've never really worked-out before. It takes consistent practice to get good at it. Practicing before you go to bed is one way of ensuring you rest well. It's all about being aware of your thoughts and feelings and letting go of the emotions attached. There is no perfect way to meditate, if you're just starting out and need one thing to focus on, start with breathing and being aware of that action. There are many guided meditation practices available for you to use on Spotify, YouTube and Netflix.

7: Sleep In Clean Bedding

Washing sheets and making up a new bed once a week may seem excessive, but it's well worth your time. Even after a few days, bed sheets can accumulate significant amounts of dust, dirt, sweat and body oils. A clean bed is a comfortable bed: A study by the National Sleep Foundation (NSF) found that people who wash their bedding and sheets regularly reported a 19% better rest at night than those who neglected the hygiene of their bedding. Think of your bed as the recharge zone to cultivate your Chi. Your bedroom should be your sanctuary - a place of quiet retreat during a busy day; a spot to unwind after work; a room to read or journal. Your bedroom should be the comfortable, calming place you look forward to resting after a long day.

8: Drop The Temperature

The temperature of your bedroom can make a substantial difference to your sleep-quality. Your body is programmed to experience a slight dip in core temperature during the evening. Turning the temperature down at night using the air-conditioning, heating systems or the use of a fan can help with temperature regulation and signal your body that it's time for bed. Melatonin is the body's natural sleep hormone and a powerful antioxidant. Your production of melatonin increases while sleeping in a cooler environment.

II.

Morning Practices

After a decent night's sleep, you're now ready to start your morning practices. These practices set you up for the morning, they're designed to improve your whole overall well-being and mental attitude for the entire day. What you do within your first couple of hours could determine the outcome of your day. Below are essential morning practices to ensure you own your morning and continue to own your day.

1: Hydration

Drinking enough water each day has many benefits. Our adult bodies are made up of around 70% water needed to regulate body temperature, keep joints lubricated, prevent infections, deliver nutrients to cells, and keep organs functioning properly. Being well-hydrated improves sleep quality, focus and mood. Start your day with hydration and steadily drink water throughout the day. How much water should you drink? This all varies with body weight and ambient conditions, rule of thumb: 2 litres for women and 2.5 litres for men is a good start. For your first drink, try a glass of warm lemon water with Himalayan salt, this can increase your immune function, decrease uric acid to fight inflammation, improve digestion and balance your body.

2: Daylight

You may be used to hearing about how too much of the sun's warm rays can be harmful to your skin. But the right balance can have lots of mood-lifting benefits. Sunlight and darkness trigger the release of hormones in your brain. Exposure to sunlight increases the brain's release of a hormone called serotonin. Serotonin is associated with boosting mood and helping you feel calm and focused. At night, a darker environment triggers the brain to make another hormone called melatonin. This hormone enhances sleeping. Without enough sun exposure, your serotonin levels can dip, this can be experienced as seasonal affective disorder or SAD syndrome. Go outside and spend ten minutes each morning soaking up the early daylight.

3: Make Your Bed

"If you want to change the world, start off by **making your bed**". - Admiral William H McRaven - US Navy.

If you make your bed every morning you would've accomplished the first task of the day. It will give you a small sense of accomplishment, which will encourage you to do another task, and another, and another and by the end of the day that one task completed would've turned into many tasks. It will make you realise that the little things do matter and if you are unable to accomplish the little things you're going to struggle to accomplish the big stuff. Making your bed sets your intentions for the day.

4: Movement

"Running water never grows stale. So you have to keep flowing". - Bruce Lee

There are many forms of exercise you can use in the morning to create movement. You may already have your own fitness goals and routine. This may be going to the gym or your pilates class. It could be simply a brisk jog or taking the dog for its morning walk. Whatever you decide to do, there is one important principle to include when you do this - that's routine and consistency each day. Exercising each day will improve your strength, fitness and endurance. It will increase energy levels and strengthen your muscles, also supporting weight loss. Exercise and movement will boost your immune system. It will better your focus, mood and overall alertness.

5: Fuel

Let's talk about nutrition briefly. We all know eating healthy is a good thing. Ensuring we actually take steps to do so is an important process in your morning. Setting yourself up with the right nutritious breakfast will enable you to focus and be ready for your day, giving you the energy you need to own your day. Skipping breakfast and relying on your coffee fix is only heading you to chronic tiredness, failing to maintain that feeling of energy throughout your day. Take the time to organise a healthy breakfast in the morning, which includes fruits, grains or slow release carbohydrates.

6: No Phone For The First Hour

You might want to workout more, you want to read more books, you want to eat healthier or you want to stop doing things less - like eating bad food, smoking or watching the news. The one thing you should do the most is stop checking your phone first thing in the morning! Why? - By checking your phone, messages, emails or Facebook and Instagram notifications, you're programming your mind to become reactive and distracted. The first hour of your day is your sacred time. If you want to own your day and become the best version of yourself, the risk is by checking your phone first thing, you are reacting to other peoples likes, shares and comments and living the first part of your day distracted by others. If you want to win the day, you need to win the first hour. These chains of habits you create are based on behaviour and your environment. If you are wanting to eat less sweets, it's best you don't have sweets in the house, right? If you want to read more, you need to set up access to more books, so your environment triggers your habits. Success will be determined by your behaviour, environment and values. Try placing your phone away from the bed or within another room, so you can't access it first thing in the morning. Manage the first hour of your day with your thoughts. You could start by writing down the three most important things you want to achieve for the day. By doing this, you will avoid the distractions and mental fatigue caused by the information overload.

III.

Goals & Affirmations

When you use daily goal setting and affirmations, it keeps your goals right where they should be: in the for-front of your mind. Using goals and affirmations will help you to condition your mind and achieve the goals you have set. Affirmations help you achieve the focus and visualisation parts of reaching your goals. Without you visualising, you will have a lesser chance of manifesting. This all starts with "I AM". Let us dive deeper into this essential daily practice.

"I AM" is the first step to setting any goal and affirmation. Whatever you wish to achieve, it's the belief and values you have towards that goal which will keep the desire and motivation alight. Let's look at some basic goal examples and affirmations to help you start off in the right direction.

Imagine you have set three goals for the next three months...

Goal One: Lose 10 kilos.

Goal Two: Spend more time with my family.

Goal Three: Save five thousand dollars for a trip to Japan.

What's important here is the affirmations behind the goals. If you don't align the right affirmations with your goals then - guess what - you'll attract the never ending need to lose ten kilos, chase the time to spend with your family and continually be saving for that trip to Japan. Let me explain: Universal law only hears what you want. So for example if you want or need to lose weight or want and need to save money then - You will always attract the need and want for these things. So what's the secret? How do you attract what you want and make a goal more obtainable? The secret is the word "I AM" gives you power towards your goals, not forgetting the values you require behind these goals, how much do you want to lose that 10kg and if you did, how would it make you feel? What would it mean to you and your family if you spent more time with them, how would they feel? How amazing it will be once you arrive in Japan, how excited are you going to be? These feelings are the fuel for motivation. Most importantly, you need to remind yourself of these goals each day so they are constantly in your subconscious space of mind continually sending out the right signals and vibrations.

Goal One: I am losing 10 kilos.

Goal Two: I am spending more time with my family.

Goal Three: I am saving five thousand dollars for a trip to Japan.

Thinking of what you want isn't enough to guarantee the results. You can supercharge these goals with affirmations to keep you in the right state of mind.

Affirmation One: I am going to the gym this morning to have an awesome workout that gets me one step closer to my weight loss goal.

Affirmation Two: I am spending time with my family, because I am a great parent and partner.

Affirmation Three: I am putting aside funds this week towards our trip to Japan that will be an amazing experience.

Affirmations are used to get you in the right state of mind for the day. Imagine, you have an interview for a new job. You set your day by starting with a good night's sleep, you have carried out your morning practices, gone over your goals and set your goals for the day. Before you head off to your important interview, you set your intentions: I am going to be great in this interview - I am going to win this job - I am going to have a successful day. By doing this, you frame your mind and energy to success. You may not always get the result you are after, however it's best to be certain that you did your best and that's what counts. By practicing affirmations, you will project better Chi, you will have better confidence and posture, you will become an action of your thoughts. For affirmations to be the most effective, they require practice and repetition throughout the day. By using this powerful tool, you will experience positive self-talk that can help you alter subconscious thoughts. Repeating a supportive, encouraging phrase gives it power, since hearing something often makes it more likely to believe. In turn, your belief makes it more likely you'll act in ways that make your affirmation become reality.

IV.

Effective VS Productive

Another essential daily practice is to understand the difference between being effective vs being productive.

If you're efficient, that means you are capable of producing desired results with little or no waste with very few resources. This is the basic dictionary definition. When we're talking about waste, we're talking about time, resources, work and materials. If you're able to produce the same amount of work with less time and resources, you're being more efficient. If you use more time and resources but produce the same amount of work as before, your performance is less efficient. Therefore, efficiency is simply the quality and degree of effectiveness at which you are being efficient. What is productive?

The dictionary defines being productive as, "having the quality or power of producing especially in abundance." Much like how "efficiency" is a measure of how efficient something or someone is, "productivity" is simply a measure of how productive you are. If you are one of those people who is focused on productivity, you'll be trying to make the most output with the resources you have. You will, for example, have a large amount of time trying to produce the largest amount of work possible or a small amount of time trying to produce the largest amount of work possible. These two concepts might sound pretty similar at first, but there is a difference when you compare them to one another. In most cases the words productivity and efficiency get thrown around as if they're the same thing. While that might be somewhat correct, it's not really correct.

There's more than meets the eye to the whole "efficiency vs. productivity". Let me explain...

Efficiency refers to the amount of effort and resources you put into your work, while productivity is all about the amount of work done over a certain period of time. Productivity is about achieving the best output, no matter the situation. Becoming more productive = more effort and more time. If you're someone who focuses on only productivity, your aim would be to accomplish everything you possibly can with what you currently have. By doing this, although you may think you are achieving more in your day, the fact is this can lead to fatigue, poor decisions and burnouts. You can be the Jack of all but you'll be the master of none. Efficiency - on the other hand -

refers to the resources used to produce that work. So, by leveraging effort and resources, you will have a more efficient process. Efficiency can also refer to the quality of the output. Building ten websites a day may look good on a productivity spreadsheet, but it's not very efficient if half of them are rejected because they don't meet quality standards. Spending hours each day trying to work out how to launch the best Facebook ads or spending hours doing your tax return may seem productive, however when the mistakes happen or the results are not what you wanted, this only eats into your time, energy and grows the frustration.

What if you were to delegate and outsource?...

What may seem unproductive or not sustainable in the beginning can be a game changer. Outsourcing can make your day become more productive and efficient, which is what you're effectively trying to achieve. Outsourcing is simply doing the things you are good at and love doing and delegating the things you are not so good at or you don't enjoy. By doing this, not only are you becoming more efficient with your time and energy, you are being more productive in the long run. If your Facebook ads are driving you insane, get someone else to do them. Yes, it's going to cost some, however if the return of investment is worth it, then you've now just freed up more time to do the things you want to do efficiently. If you don't enjoy grocery shopping, order online deliveries. If you suck at cleaning, hire a cleaner. You could use the additional time to generate further income doing the things you love. At the end of the day, you are aiming to apply small changes to eliminate the frustrations and increase the joy, harmony and happiness within your work and home. When you focus on being efficient, it will free up more of your time and help you cultivate your energy.

V.

Jets On - Jets Off

Taking time out each day is vital for productivity in whatever you are striving to achieve and an essential practice to ensure you own your day. When you want to move forwards with your goals and intentions, it's important to fire the jets "ON" and head in the direction that you are aiming for... we know this... but what some of us can take for granted, is the importance of Jets "OFF".

So many of us are caught in the grind of work, family responsibilities and ongoing stress. Often, we only allow ourselves to truly rest on holidays or leave. However, it's so important to prioritise proper rest and quality sleep in your everyday life. Rest and sleep are two different things. We understand the importance of sleep, but both are equally important to your mental, emotional and physical health. Prioritising "Jets off" can actually improve your quality of sleep. "Jets off" can be difficult to define because it can look different for everyone. "Jets off" is any behaviour aimed at increasing physical or mental well-being. It can be active, such as going for a walk outside, or passive, such as taking ten minutes to sit down and breathe deeply. Regardless of how you choose to do this, these daily behaviours can help you recover and recharge from physical and mental effort. If you ignore your body signals and prevent short periods of rest, long-term stress could take effect, leading to pains, headaches, digestive issues, anxiety, ability to focus and even depression. It may not seem like a big deal to skip relaxation in your daily routine. However, there are several benefits to daily "Jets off" and resting:

- reduced stress and anxiety
- improved mood
- decreased blood pressure
- chronic pain relief
- improved immune health
- stronger cardiovascular system

So, how can you better prioritise "Jets off"? Find small ways in which you can incorporate rest and reset into your daily routine. You make time every day to eat, take your kids to school, do errands and go to work. Why should rest be any different? Start by finding a relaxation technique that works for you. This could be meditating, exercise, walking outside, listening to music, reading a book, drinking tea or any combination of these things. When planning out your daily schedule, find a consistent time for "Jets off".

Recharging your mind, body and soul can give you great benefits to your Jets "ON" time. You should know that some of the most successful people in this world spend up to 4 hours each morning before their day starts, valuing this Jets "OFF" time in order to be more efficient when it counts and prevent the endless amount of time wasted, either sitting in front of a computer or trying to complete tasks without a fully focused mind.

JETS ON when it counts, JETS OFF for efficiency = less wasted time.

VI.

Mother of Motivation

How do you create motivation? You can't suddenly feel motivated any more than you can feel suddenly happy. Happiness is the result of a thought, not an impulse. It's in your mind that you experience something at the time that brings you joy. A long lasting sense of happiness comes from practice of positive memories and choice of thought. Once you understand this, you realise that motivation is a choice and a commitment to be motivated towards something that you deeply desire. It is an energy resulting from your thoughts. You will feel motivated from within from a conscious choice. Imagine feeling empowered with motivation every day. Imagine being able to use this power to take action on every goal you wish to achieve. Imagine if you were able to turn this motivation on like a light switch. If you could do this, do you think it would be far easier to achieve things? Motivation is simply your thoughts transcended into actions. Let me share with you this process to use, to continuously enhance the power of your motivation.

Visualise Ambition

When you are ambitious, you are striving to achieve something great. The thoughts of your ambitions could include something like winning a sports league championship. You may want to master an instrument and play in a renowned concert. You may have ambitions to purchase your first property or even a portfolio of properties. You may decide to have ambitions to become a successful actor or actress. Whatever they are, you choose your ambitions based on the excitement and value they give you. It's an exciting moment when you decide to visualise your ambitions. It can be like looking into life's catalog of desires. No goal should be too big and no goal too small. Ambitions are a healthy way to visualise the goals needed for you to start the motive towards them.

Feel The Desire

Desire is the strong feeling you have towards an ambition or goal you wish to achieve. It is said, that without desire you will lack the spark of motivation. This feeling should be a deep and meaningful purpose to which you will stop at nothing to achieve it. The stronger the desire, the stronger the motivation. Your goal may be to travel more or to spend more time with family. Your goal may be to one day quit your current job and start your own business. In any case, it's not specifically your goal that determines the desire, however it's important to ensure the purpose of your goal triggers an emotional responsibility. It's this responsibility that cements the burning desire to achieve what you want in life.

Ignite The Spark

Once you have visualised what you want and the feelings that are associated with these ambitions, it's time to ignite the spark! That spark of motivation you are looking for is not going to come directly from anything external. It's not going to come from your coach, your friends or your family. This spark is living in you. What's required is your thoughts and visualisations to trigger the emotional state that sparks motivation. This could be as simple as a weight loss goal. Looking at an old picture of yourself in your prime. Imagining the wedding you want on that tropical island. Visualising two hands on the wheel of the sports car you've always wanted to drive. By combining visualisations and emotions, you will be able to spark motivation at any given time.

Ditch Discipline Justify Self-worth

Discipline can be a harsh word. When we think of being disciplined, it can almost feel like a punishment. I'm sure you have tried forms of discipline when it came to something important for you. Sticking to something that requires you to force and action cannot be tolerated or sustained for long. Instead of discipline, try using self-worth. Self-worth is the internal sense of being good enough and worthy of the things you love. By shifting your thoughts to self-worth each time you feel the need to be disciplined, you will find that the desire to achieve your goals is deeper than the task. If you are worth it, you deserve to achieve it.

Give It Attention

Despite all the right motives, if you don't give something your full attention, you will never see it grow. Your goals and ambitions require consistent attention. Just the thought alone will only get you so far. It's easy to run out of motivation for something that seems so far out of reach, however with constant actions each day and continuous thought, you will eventually see the fruits of your labour. It's like anything you wish to be great at or achieve. Michael Jordan was the greatest basketball player not for his skill alone, but to develop this skill, he gave each practice session his full attention. After practice was over, he would practice again. To be the best at something, requires an obsession to consistently place your full focus and attention to it. The more you focus, the more you put into it, the better you will become.

Just Take The First Step

Like it or not, in order for you to achieve something great, you must take the first step. Your first step is the most important one of all, because it sets you up for momentum. There may have been a time in your life when you wanted something and you procrastinated in the moment. There may have been a time in your life when you had ambition and dreams that were crushed by fear and self-doubt. You won't get it perfect, you won't have all the answers. Take the first step, action now, questions later and learn along the way. 90% is still an A. Once you take the first step, you'll feel motivated to take the next.

Amplify With Your Surroundings

Your surroundings play an important influence in your life, your goals and your motivation. It has been said that you will become the average of the five people you associate with the most. This being said, it's important to surround yourself with self-motivated people. Do the people around you build you up? Or are they energy zappers? When you surround yourself with the right people and influences, you will feel your motivation amplify!

Fear Or Freedom

Fear is a primal motivator. If you can remember being in a fearful situation, something that scared or terrified you, that motivation to escape can be a powerful emotion. Likewise by turning your motivation to a source of freedom, that sense of freedom that people fought for, the ability to have more options in your life financially, freedom to travel, freedom to live life in abundance or in a peaceful and carefree manner, you can use this freedom as a primal motivator. We are either motivated by fear or freedom.

VII.

Meaning of Life

"You are not a person experiencing life, you are life experiencing it as a person.

We are energy" - Mark Kien Sin

Find your purpose

Instead of looking for the true meaning of life, many seek meaning in other people; they believe it may free them from their emptiness. In reality, the only thing that can fill this void is to find your own true purpose. This means that when you have a reason to live, no matter if you are focusing on the love you have for another person or a goal you want to achieve, you can face almost any circumstance. That being said, this journey will not go without a degree of discomfort in order for you to grow. You associate the feeling of discomfort with something you do not want, but you should do – such as having surgery. It may be necessary, but it certainly is not comfortable. Inner growth is somewhat similar. Leaving your comfort zone and discovering your life purpose may not be pleasant at first. Although there is a certain amount of frustration, these feelings are essentially beneficial. They show that you are on the way to discovering your true meaning. Therefore, despite any discomfort you feel, work hard to find out what will give you that sense of accomplishment and true meaning. You may not know what this purpose is yet, you may be feeling lost and unclear. Understand that this is part of the process and as long as you continue to search for it, it will unfold for you, (sometimes when you least expect it). When you find your purpose you will give and gain happiness in harmony.

Express yourself

You are the artist of your own life. If you were given a blank canvas, what would you paint? The ability to truly express yourself comes from a sense of being secure in yourself. Security and a thick skin comes from knowing who you are, and what you stand for. Expression is greatest when it evolves from a place of authenticity, heart, and love. It can be challenging to truly express yourself. This can be due to fear, not knowing who you truly are, or not even knowing how. You may often try to fit in among the crowd. This fitting in causes inner confusion. Confusion between WHO YOU ARE vs. WHO YOU ARE TRYING TO BE. You may often do things because OTHERS do it, NOT necessarily because YOU like to do it. You must discover who you are and gain self-awareness to learn how to express yourself. Once you do so, self-expression has the power to transform your life. You can then live your life in alignment with who you are, and authentically express it to the world.

Create moments

In your life there are memories and moments. These stay with you for as long as you live and live on with others. The experiences created from these moments make up who you are and what you believe in. Everyone has a unique path that unfolds. Some events are out of your control and others are by choice. It's the choice that matters, for what you choose is your responsibility and for what you may feel out of your control should only build you up, for life does not happen to you, it happens for you. Look back only to see how far you've come knowing that you can only join the dots backwards. You are in the exact place you need to be right now and have the power to choose the next chapter. Life is a bunch of moments put together over time.

Be present

In this fast-paced world we live in, where everything happens so fast and everything becomes obsolete so quickly, most of us have forgotten to be present, to fully enjoy the moment. If you are present in a moment, you are listening to others, being aware of your surroundings, and engaging with those around you. By being present you are aware of the moment you're in rather than reliving past moments or worrying about the future. It is the moment when you are calm and you know exactly what you want. You are focused on what you're doing without thinking about anything else. That's when life is more real.

Embrace suffering

To embrace suffering you must look at your circumstances with loving kindness, compassion, and mindfulness, and find ways to embrace the suffering by looking deeply into it. Suffering is unavoidable. It's a part of life. It becomes a part of your life forever, when you try to avoid it. When you choose to run away from your pain and suffering, without accepting it and experiencing it the way it is, it gets difficult to overcome. Nothing works best to overcome the pain, then the acceptance. Once you accept what is present in the moment, you can move in the direction of achievement. It's only when you accept the events of the past and give all your energy in healing the pain, you can overcome any pain or suffering in your life. With understanding and compassion, you will be able to heal the wounds in your heart, and the wounds in the world.

Take responsibility

When you are not sure of the meaning of life, you may begin to ask others. It's a common question and it's a difficult question to answer because it varies from person to person. You will have to live your own mission in life, and only you can discover it and fulfil it. This all revolves around taking responsibility for your own actions, for where you are right now, no matter how good or bad your situation is, you must understand that it was a result of your actions. It may be difficult to comprehend because life tends to deal us different cards. What's important is knowing that the moment you accept responsibility for where you are right now, is the moment you can change your life for the better.

Lessons are learned from circumstances

Every experience you live, gives you the opportunity to learn. Life will have its ups and downs. The aim is not to fear the unknown, but to accept it and grow from it. By having the determination to survive and to be focused on future goals you dream of achieving, you will not allow your circumstances to dictate your outcome in life. Your life will have purpose, your life will have meaning, and in the toughest situations you will refuse to give up. When you have a real reason to live, you will find ways to manage your circumstances.

Love and be loved

One way to find meaning in your life is to love others. Sincere and deep love can help you in the worst situations. Loving someone and being loved can also be a sense of purpose in life. It is said that someone who has nothing left to lose – no identity, possessions or money – can still have a reason to live and experience happiness, if they think of someone they love. Contemplating a loved one during difficult times can help you to avoid the existential emptiness, giving meaning and fulfilment, even when it seems you have nothing. We will all face difficult times in our lives. Concentrating on the love you have for someone else can help you stay focused and keep you from losing hope in yourself, in your life and in humanity.

Live life as if you were living it for the second time

This affirmation can stimulate your sense of responsibility by encouraging you to imagine that the present has already happened, therefore gaining the benefit of a different perspective from your life. By living as if you were granted that new life now, you can make better decisions. Imagine that the life that you are living now is the second or a new life. If you think like that, then you will come to realise your past actions. You will endeavour to become the best version of yourself. Life can be lived with passion, purpose, love and happiness. Life can be lived with kindness and compassion. Life can be lived with peace and harmony.

"Live life as if you were living it for the second time."

Holistic Feng Shui

Holistic Feng Shui is about thinking and living in your true values of life. By using the teachings in this book, you will now have the basics to get you started on a life that's clutter free and flowing with good Chi. You will be able to create a life of fulfillment, balance and happiness. You will accept your struggles and be motivated to solve them. You will discover your purpose and be focused on achieving it. By using the practices and making small changes each day, you will become more clear on your goals, more productive and a happier person. Your vibration will attract more and more happiness into your life. Amongst the chaos you now have the cure and the secret of Chi. Like anything you want to be great at, it will require effort, attention and practice. It's important to not compare yourself to someone else but to compare yourself to who you were Yesterday and make it your mission to become better each day. Be aware of your thoughts, attract what you want in life. Live in a space that influences ambitions and helps you find the peace, joy and happiness you deserve.

Seven Daily Practices To Own Your Day

I. Start With Sleep

II. Morning Practices

III. Goals & Affirmations

IV. Effective VS Productive

V. Jets On - Jets Off

VI. Mother of Motivation

VII. Meaning of Life

About The Author

Mark Kien Sin Lupo, the author behind this book was born and raised in London, England. He came from a family background of Asian and European parents. There was something that always stood out in his life, health and fitness and an obsession to keep his space clean and clutter free, this could be his room, car - you name it. Everything had to have its purpose and place. He always had a hunger to keep his life healthy and in order. At the age of 28, he immigrated to Australia to explore a new circle of influences and widen his perception on life. After finishing up his career in electrical engineering, his mission was to work on his true purpose, something he would find fulfillment in. Health and wellness became his passion and a lifestyle. From this point of his life, he was dedicated to become a fitness and life coach and helped hundreds of clients become the best versions of themselves. Over the next decade, he went on to create a small group fitness gym, helping clients achieve sustainable approaches to their health and lifestyle goals. He made an appearance on Channel seven, sharing the power of vision boards after using this method and making several of his own life goals become reality. A few years later he created and became the founder of Hang Tuff, the first suspension training studio in Western Australia. Personal development became his priority, reading dozens of books, it was the quest for knowledge and the investment in himself that became a huge value to his life. After diving into the world of Feng Shui, he found synergy between a positive mindset and positive spaces. As we all experience, there are times in life that are filled with fear, doubt and uncertainty and one of the most important things for him to be able to regain focus was to be productive and happy by working on a healthy mindset and allowing good energy to flow within his space. That's how Holistic Feng Shui was born and became the solution. Now, as a qualified Feng Shui consultant, fitness and life coach, living and practicing this knowledge during times of chaos has been fundamental for a life of greater peace and harmony. During this time he started writing this book, realising Feng Shui and the years of personal development had a deep connection and a secret that needed to be shared.

Finding your purpose will allow you to continually evolve into the best version of yourself." - Mark Kien Sin

MARK KIEN SIN

HOLISTIC FENG SHUI

The Feng Shui colour chart

COLOUR	ELEMENT	SYMBOLISUM	BAUGUA AREA	USE
WHITE	METAL	CLEANINESS, OPENESS AND PURITY	CREATIVITY, CONTRIBUTION AND TRAVEL	KITCHEN AND BEDROOMS
BLUE	WATER	SERENITY	MEDITATION, DEPENDABILITY AND CAREER	BEDROOMS AND BATHROOMS
BLACK	WATER	STRENTH, INDEPENDANCE AND MYSTICAL	KNOWLEDGE, CAREER AND POWER	BEDROOM FOR ADULTS OR TEENS
GREEN	WOOD	GROWTH AND HARMONY	FERTILITY, HEALTH AND FAMILY	BATHROOMS
YELLOW	EARTH	UPLIFTING, HAPPY AND SOCIAL	FAME, RELATIONSHIPS AND FREINDSHIPS	KITCHEN, LIVING AND DINING ROOM
RED	FIRE	STIMULATION	PASSION, FAME, PROSPERITY AND LOVE	ADULT BEDROOM, TONE/KITCHEN DINNING
ORANGE	FIRE	ACTIVE, CHEERFUL AND SOCIAL	FAME, ABUNDANCE AND REPUTATION	LIVING AND DINING ROOM
PINK	FIRE	HAPPINESS AND PURE THOUGHTS	LOVE AND ROMANCE	BEDROOM
PURPLE	WOOD	DIGNITY, GRACE, SPIRITUALITY AND SENSUALITY	CALMING, PROSPERITY, WEALTH AND LUCK	BEDROOMS, SHADES/LIVING ROOM
GOLD	METAL	PROSPERITY	WEALTH AND SPIRITUALITY	ACCENTS AND ACCESSORIES
GREY	METAL	NEUTRAL, CALM AND STILLNESS	KNOWLEDGE, CREATIVITY, CONTRIBUTION	UNDERTONE OR ACCENTS
BROWN	EARTH	GROUNDING AND MATERNAL	STABILITY AND CAREER	LIVING ROOM

The Feng Shui Bagua Map

WEALTH, PROSPERITY & SELF-WORTH WOOD PURPLE, GOLD	FAME, REPUTATION & SOCIAL LIFE FIRE RED, ORANGE	MARRIAGE AND RELATIONSHIPS EARTH PINK, SKIN AND EARTH TONES
HEALTH, FAMILY AND COMMUNITY WOOD GREEN, GOLD	GOOD FORTUNE CENTER EARTH YELLOW, EARTH TONES	CHILDREN, CREATIVITY AND FUN METAL WHITE, BRIGHT, PASTEL
WISDOM, & SELF-KNOWLEDGE EARTH BLUE, GREEN	CAREER, LIFE MISSION & INDIVIDUALITY WATER BLACK, DARK BLUES	HELP, CONTRIBUTION, SPIRIT AND TRAVEL METAL GRAYS, SILVER

The Feng Shui Elements Charts

Element	Creates	Weakens	Destroys
FIRE	EARTH	WOOD	METAL
EARTH	METAL	FIRE	WATER
METAL	WATER	EARTH	WOOD
WATER	WOOD	METAL	FIRE
WOOD	FIRE	WATER	EARTH

Element	Energy	Yin Or Yang
WATER	Adaptation - Flow	Yin
EARTH	Softness - Purity - Growth	Yin
WOOD	Dark - Bold - Thunder	Yang
WOOD	Light - Flowing - Serene	Yin
EARTH	Centre of Collective Energy	
METAL	Strong - Heavy - Hevenly - Unbendable	Yang
METAL	Soft - Flexible - Reflection	Yin
EARTH	Strong - Solid - Scenic - Mountains	Yang
FIRE	Smart - Impulsive - Energetic	Yang

Printed in Great Britain
by Amazon